The 90-Minute Resume

The 90-Minute Resume

Peggy Schmidt

Peterson's Guides
Princeton, New Jersey

Library of Congress Cataloging-in-Publication Data
Schmidt, Peggy J.
     The 90-minute resume / Peggy Schmidt.
          p.   cm.
     ISBN 0-87866-997-3
     1. Resumes (Employment). 2. Applications for positions.
  I. Title. II. Title: Ninety-minute resume.
  HF5383.S325   1990
  650.1'4—dc20   89-71000
                                                              CIP

Composition and design by Peterson's Guides

Printed in the United States of America

10 9 8 7 6 5 4 3 2 1

Contents

(continued)

Preface

After my book *Making It on Your First Job: When You're Young, Inexperienced and Ambitious* came out nine years ago, relatives and friends—and friends of friends—began asking me to help them put together or revise their resume. The approach I used and refined over time was based on my years of experience and training as a journalist: I asked the job hunter questions in the same way I would if I'd been interviewing him or her for an article. The technique seemed to work no matter who I was helping—my brother, a recent college graduate; a friend who had worked in one profession for ten years but wanted to change careers; my mother, who was going back to work after a twenty-five-year hiatus. "You made me look great!" they told me. They got interviews and they landed good jobs.

I began passing along the highlights of my interview technique to students at the New York University Summer Publishing Institute, where I'm the career coordinator. I've reviewed hundreds of resumes since 1982 and have seen dramatic improvements after students followed my suggestions. Many have told me that they felt much more confident about starting their job search because they knew their resume portrayed them at their best.

A year and a half ago, I decided to self-publish my "interview approach" to resume writing and offer it to readers of the weekly column I write for New York's *Daily News*, "Your New Job." Hundreds wrote in to ask for a copy, and some of those called back to say that after following the guide they'd received compliments on their resume from the employers they'd interviewed with.

That prompted me to restudy the resume books on my bookshelf and the latest releases in bookstores. I found they were thick with sample resumes and jammed with self-assessment exercises, but short on the kind of advice that I considered really helpful. Maybe, I told myself, more people than I'd originally thought could benefit from *The 90-Minute Resume.*

This book grew out of the original guide, expanded and revised according to the suggestions of readers who had developed resumes with that first version. I owe them many thanks for their recommendations.

I'm the kind of person who would like to play the role of interviewer with every job hunter who needs help with his or her resume. Since I can't do that, I'm honored that you've decided to have me as the unseen muse who, I hope, will inspire you and your interviewer to produce a truly outstanding resume.

Peggy Schmidt
November 1989

Introduction

I recently went to the Improvisation, a famous comedy club in New York City, and had the luck to land a front-row seat and exchange friendly barbs with a talented comedian. If you've ever been to such a club, you're familiar with the comedian's routine: "Hello, there. What's your name? What do you do for a living?"

When I mentioned that I was a writer who had a book called *The 90-Minute Resume* coming out, he asked, "Who's it for?"

"It's not for comedians," I replied.

"Not for comedians," he gasped, disbelievingly. "You don't think we need to work? You think every club owner we contact wants to hire us?"

I was wrong—he was right. *The 90-Minute Resume* is for anyone who needs to present his or her credentials on paper. Whether you're an experienced professional, someone who wants to change careers or industries, a recent college graduate, or someone who is returning to work after taking time off for school or for personal or family reasons, *The 90-Minute Resume* can help you create a positive, winning profile. And creating or improving a resume isn't as overwhelming or as time-consuming a task as you might imagine.

In the course of my career, I've had the opportunity to compare thousands of resumes and have given suggestions to hundreds of job seekers about how to make theirs better. In the process, I learned five important things:

1. Candidates with similar credentials can come across as more or less qualified depending on what they say or don't say—and how well they say it.
2. It is possible to present yourself as a terrific job candidate without telling white lies, no matter how limited or interrupted your job experience

1

is or how much less than top-notch your credentials are.

3. You can communicate your skills and experience effectively on paper even if you are not a good writer.
4. How well you present yourself in a resume can result in your being asked in for an interview—or being deep-sixed in a file cabinet.
5. Job hunters who are changing fields or industries stand a better chance of being considered if their resumes are conceived with prospective employers' needs in mind.

I know what you're thinking—"That's great, but now I'm more nervous than ever about doing a good job." You needn't be. Making your resume the best it can be isn't difficult, nor does it need to be time-consuming.

Think of a resume as you would a coming attraction for a movie; if the feature piques your interest, you're likely to see it when it is released. Similarly, an enticing resume can win you a call for an interview from a prospective employer. What makes for an enticing resume? First, it must be visually inviting. Second, it should highlight your experiences and skills in an easy-to-follow format. Third, and perhaps most important, it should point to the results of your efforts, not just provide descriptions of the jobs you've held.

While there are no hard-and-fast rules about how long a resume should be, one page is ideal. Why? Because most people, with the exception of academics, scientists, and medical doctors, can adequately summarize their experience in that space. Because employers are looking for highlights, not details, and often prefer one-page resumes. Because a resume that's longer than one page has the inherent physical problem of staying attached—staples aren't infallible.

You can create a great resume in a relatively short period of time by using the method that I've developed from years of teaching resume-writing workshops and working with individuals to perfect their resumes. I've found it to be not only the quickest but also the best way to get experience and skills down on paper; it's called the interview method.

How does it work? Find a person, someone who is familiar with your background and who, preferably, already has had the experience of putting together a resume or is currently doing so, to play the role of **interviewer.** That person might be a spouse, friend, former colleague, classmate, parent, brother, or sister. The job of the interviewer (that's how he or she will be referred to throughout the book) is to ask you, the **job hunter** (that's how you'll be referred to), questions about your education, work experience, activities, skills, and interests.

This book contains all the information the two of you need to produce a resume that will portray you at your best. Before you schedule an interview time, be sure to skim through *The 90-Minute Resume* to get an idea of how it works. There are several things you'll want to prepare in advance; these are discussed in the section called "First, Your Fact Sheets," on page 11. It's also a good idea for the interviewer to familiarize himself or herself with the process. A quick read-through of the book is the best way, but if your interviewer doesn't have the time, have him or her read "Tips for the Interviewer" on page 5.

Finally, keep this thought in mind as you work: Believe in yourself. Even if you think that you've done only ordinary things, you are a special person with unique experiences and skills. You *can* get a good first job or find a better job than you now have. Go into the interview session with the conviction that the resume you will create is the first step in a new direction. You'll be able to answer your interviewer's questions more confidently, and that will translate into a stronger resume.

An hour and a half is a realistic time period in which to produce a working copy—one that needs only to be retyped—if you're willing to keep socializing to a minimum and working to a maximum. So turn off the radio, order some pizza (there *is* a break that is not included in the 90 minutes), and let's get started!

Tips for the Interviewer

Your responsibility as interviewer is to elicit as much information about the job hunter's background as possible—information that will later be used to construct or revise a resume. Interviewer guidelines are interspersed throughout the book to assist you, and the questions for you to ask are laid out in the different sections of the book. You should feel free, however, to improvise whenever you think it's necessary to get relevant information. You'll also be able to take cues from the fact sheets the job hunter has filled out. Keep in mind the following:

1. *Be encouraging.* Most people feel uncomfortable talking about themselves and their accomplishments, so be sure to put the job hunter at ease by being a good listener and complimenting his or her answers.

2. *Don't hesitate to probe.* If you don't understand something the job hunter has said, ask for an explanation. Why? Because the employer who is reading the job hunter's resume is likely to be confused too, if the same words are used on paper. Also, people have the tendency to simplify or gloss over accomplishments that deserve more attention. So be sure to ask, "Wasn't that above and beyond the call of duty?"

3. *Get details.* Job hunters too often preedit their experiences because they want to get everything down on one page. Your job is to draw out specifics—in particular, numbers, percentages, and amounts that quantify skills and accomplishments. The two of you can decide later which facts to include.

4. *Take notes.* It's difficult for the job hunter to write while speaking, so as you listen, jot down key words and phrases that sound important to you. Before moving on to the next question, read back what you've got. If you have suggestions for a more effective word or phrase, suggest it.

5. *Direct the conversation.* Part of your job is to keep the interview on track. Don't let the job hunter stray from the question you've asked; simply say, "That's good information, but save it for later because I'll be asking about it." And keep in mind that no one question should take more than a few minutes to answer. If it does, the two of you won't be able to produce a working copy in the 90 minutes allotted.

Sharpen your investigative reporting instincts and your pencil, and get ready. The role you are about to play in helping the job hunter get that good job is an important one.

Creating Your Resume "From Scratch"

If you're a working person who wants to present your credentials in a fresh way, a student, a recent graduate, or a parent returning to the job market, a good way to approach resume writing is "from scratch." Starting with the basics allows the greatest flexibility in deciding the content and format of your resume.

To begin, the more you know about the kind of position you want or the field you hope to get into, the easier the job of organizing the information from the interview session. Let's say, for example, that you've held a variety of secretarial and administrative assistant jobs and you hope to land a position in which you could get paralegal training. It would be in your best interest to stress your researching, proofreading, and writing skills, since they're essential to the job of a paralegal.

Be sure to let your interviewer know what your plans are, and familiarize him or her with the types of skills and experiences a particular job or field requires so that the questions asked can be more direct.

If you're open to a variety of positions, you'll want to emphasize the range of skills and knowledge that you've acquired rather than focus on ones that would help you land a particular type of job.

Time for this exercise: 10 minutes

First, Your Fact Sheets

Before you sit down with your interviewer, it's a good idea to put the following headings on separate pieces of blank paper. We'll call them your fact sheets.

Identification

Work Experience

Education

Activities

Interests

Fill in factual information under the appropriate headings in advance so that the interviewer will be able to quiz you more effectively—and quickly. If you have a typewriter or, better yet, a computer and word processing software, use it to type in this preliminary information on the fact sheets.

First, fill out the identification fact sheet. It's very simple—just put your name (a formal name rather than a nickname), address (include street number and name, apartment number, city, state, and zip code), and phone number, including area code.

If you have more than one address because you're a student or someone who lives away from home part of the year, indicate which one is your permanent address. You might also want to include the dates you can be reached at both addresses as the last line of information in this section.

The phone number must be one where you, or someone who can take a message for you, are available during working hours. If there are times when no one is home, consider investing in an answering machine or a message pickup service. List only your work number if you can comfortably accept a phone call, however brief, from a prospective employer.

Now, let's move on to your work experience fact sheet. For each job you've held, starting with the most recent, list:

- Your job title(s), the employer's name and location (city and state), dates of employment (month and year)

EXAMPLE

Engineering drafter, Computech, Inc., Norwood, Massachusetts, June 1984–September 1986

Include internships, summer jobs (if you're a student or recent grad), and part-time and unpaid job experiences, as well as full-time positions.

EXAMPLES

Publicity intern, WNET-TV, New York, New York, Summer 1989

Switchboard operator, Fort Lauderdale City Hall, Fort Lauderdale, Florida, September 1988–August 1989

On your education fact sheet:

- Name of high school, month and year of graduation (if you've already graduated from college, this information isn't necessary)
- Name of vocational, trade, or technical school; month and year of graduation; name of program completed (if applicable)

- Name of degree received; major; name of college; dates of attendance or month and year of graduation; graduation honors; grade or grade point average if at the B level or better; names of special courses or programs you took abroad, during summer school, or at a specialized school; dates of attendance; certificates or special recognition received. (Note: If you haven't yet graduated, simply put: Candidate, name of degree, date of expected graduation.)

EXAMPLES

College graduate: Bachelor of Arts, Government, University of Arizona, April 1988
  —Cum laude
  —Harry S. Truman scholarship ($7,000 award based on B average and ranking in upper quartile of class)

Some college education: Full-time student, Ohio University, September 1984–December 1986
  —Financed 80 percent of college education with 30-hour-a-week job

On your activities fact sheet:

- Name of clubs, organizations, teams, professional organizations in which you were an active participant; your role; dates of membership

EXAMPLES

Rainforest Action Movement, publicity coordinator, 1988–89

Summit Ice Hockey Team, goalie, 1986–89

An activities section on your resume is optional. If you're not currently involved in any because of the demands of your current job or for family or personal reasons, don't worry. However, listing activities can support your case if they involve skills that are needed in the job you're applying for. If they aren't work related, they can add insight into the kind of person you are. One caveat: If you're involved in controversial social or political activities, a pro-life or pro-choice group, for example, you're better off omitting your involvement. A prospective employer may have different views on the issue, and including yours could interfere with your being considered for a job.

As with the activities section, the interests section is optional. But unless you are a couch potato, it's a good idea to include it—at the beginning of the interview a prospective employer often starts with questions about your interests as an icebreaker. And if you and the employer share similar interests, it can help you clinch the job.

On your interests fact sheet:

- A short list of activities you enjoy doing in your free time

EXAMPLE

Listening to big-band jazz, whale watching, candlepin bowling

Time for this exercise: Total time:
30 minutes 40 minutes

Ready, Set, Start the Interview

The whole point of having the interviewer ask you questions is to have you talk about your work and educational background, which is much easier than writing about it. It's the interviewer's job to ask, "Explain what you mean," or "Can you give me an example?" if he or she doesn't understand your answer. Try to use words that clearly and simply describe your job responsibilities, skills, and accomplishments. Avoid using jargon and technical terms.

Keep a pen or pencil in hand at all times; you'll want to jot down words, phrases, and well-expressed ideas as soon as you've answered a question to your interviewer's satisfaction. The interviewer can help by noting key words and phrases as you speak. Taking good notes will make it easier for you to write your resume.

If you have a tape recorder, you may want to tape your session. It will allow you to rewind and play back parts of the Q and A—particularly if something brilliant is said and promptly forgotten.

The interviewer should have your fact sheets in front of him or her. Let's assume for the moment that your identification fact sheet is fine and start with the work experience fact sheet. When answering the interviewer's questions, try to use numbers, percentages, and amounts to describe how many, how often, or how much. Quantifying

15

what you've done and what you know helps put your accomplishments and skills into perspective for the employer who will be reviewing your resume.

Interviewer guideline: Start with the most recently held job and work backward. If the job hunter has already given some thought to what he or she does on the job and what his or her accomplishments have been, you may not need to go beyond the first two questions for each job. The additional questions are suggestions of what to ask if you need to dig deeper. Remember to spend more time (up to 5 minutes) on those that relate to the kind of position the job hunter hopes to find. If you haven't already discussed the job hunter's plans, do it now. If you're not familiar with the requirements of the position the job hunter hopes to win, ask about them.

Keep in mind that in addition to having the job hunter clearly describe his or her responsibilities, the person must also discuss accomplishments. Everyone has some, even if they don't immediately come to mind. So don't take "I can't think of any" for an answer.

Treat all kinds of work experience—paid, volunteer, part-time, or full-time—in the same way. If the job hunter hasn't had much work experience or experience directly related to the kind of work he or she is applying for, it's particularly important to encourage the person to talk about what he or she has learned and contributed.

Finally, jot down the verbs, not the "responsible for"s, in the job hunter's answers. If you can suggest more descriptive words, do so.

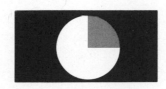

Time for this exercise:
15 minutes

Work Experience Questions

- What exactly did you do on your job on a regular (daily, weekly, or monthly) basis? Start with the tasks you consider most important and try to come up with at least five, even if you don't include all of them in your final resume.
- Did any of your accomplishments ever result in a promotion, raise, or other type of recognition? Please describe them and quantify with numbers, for example, a *10 percent* bonus or a *doubling* of your client list.
- Did you manage the work of one or more employees? If so, how many? At what level (clerical, technical, senior staff, etc.) were those employees?
- What are some of the most important projects you worked on? Briefly describe their purpose and your role. Did you meet or exceed the expectations of your boss (or management)?
- Did you suggest an idea that was successfully implemented by your boss, department, or company? Please describe what it involved, your role in making it work, and any credit or compliments you received as a result.
- Did you train one or more employees to do something you know how to do well? Describe the nature of the task or tasks, whether you did it on your own initiative, and whether others learned how to do it successfully.

- What have you done that has made you feel satisfied or won praise from your boss, management, or clients?

Interviewer guideline: If the job hunter can't come up with anything, ask how he or she handled an emergency or crisis situation or functioned on the job when the boss wasn't around and whether he or she was complimented on job performance during a review.

• • • •

SAMPLE CONVERSATION

Interviewer: What exactly did you do as a production assistant at WPIX-TV?

Job Hunter: Probably the most important thing I did every day was to check into daily news bulletins and write rough copy for the evening news and weekly magazine programs.

Interviewer: What do you mean when you say "checked into"?

Job Hunter: I called up the sources who were mentioned to verify and add information to what was in the bulletin.

Interviewer: How many news bulletins did you check into every day?

Job Hunter: At least a dozen.

Interviewer: What do you mean by "rough copy"?

Job Hunter: A writer and an editor would usually take what I wrote up and polish it.

What to write down:
- Checked into a dozen news bulletins daily.
- Called up sources to verify and add information.

- Wrote rough copy for writers and editors to polish.

Unless you're still enrolled in school or are a recent graduate, your education section should follow the work experience section. (If you are still a student, however, the education section should lead off the body of your resume.) So let's tackle the education fact sheet next.

Interviewer guideline: Start by reading over the information on the education fact sheet. Ask questions about anything that is unclear to you, even if it's a simple detail about the type of degree or certificate received.

Time for this exercise:
5 minutes

Education Questions

- Did you work to put yourself through school? If so, what percentage of your education did you pay for?

Interviewer guideline: If the job hunter has listed any information beyond the name of the degree earned, the program or school, and dates of attendance, ask the following questions.

- How were you selected for the honor, scholarship, or award you've listed? Was it based on grades, leadership ability, or involvement in school organizations? Who made the decision—faculty, administration, officers of the awarding organization, your peers?

- Were others selected or were you the only one?
- Was there a cash award involved? If so, how much?

• • • •

SAMPLE CONVERSATION

Interviewer: You've written down that you received an honor for outstanding academic achievement. What exactly did you do?

Job Hunter: I wrote a term paper that was cited as one of the ten best written by a senior.

Interviewer: That's terrific, especially because good writing skills are a requirement for the position you're applying for. Did someone nominate you for it?

Job Hunter: My history professor submitted it as the best term paper from his department.

Interviewer: Did other departments enter submissions?

Job Hunter: All twenty departments in the arts and sciences division competed. A faculty committee made the decision from among the finalists.

Interviewer: Do you know how many term papers were considered?

Job Hunter: My professor told me it was over 300.

What to write down:
- Wrote one of ten best senior term papers.
- Nominated by history professor.
- Selected by a faculty committee from a field of 20 finalists and over 300 entrants.

Now let's go on to the activities fact sheet.

Interviewer guideline: If the job hunter is a student or recent graduate, concentrate on extracurricular activities that relate to the type of job he or she hopes to land. If the job hunter is returning to the job market after managing a family and a household, club and organization experience is important because many of the skills used in these activities will transfer to a work situation.

Time for this exercise:
5 minutes

Activities Questions

- Were you involved in any special activities, committees, or fund-raising as a member? Describe what you did and use numbers to quantify where you can.
- Were you an elected or appointed officer of the club or organization? If so, did you serve as a representative of your group? To whom did you represent it?

Interviewer guideline: If the type of organization is not obvious from the name, ask:
- What kind of organization is the XYZ club—social, professional, community, student government, or other type of special interest group?

• • • •

SAMPLE CONVERSATION

Interviewer: You say that you've built a multitrack home sound recording and video studio. What have you used it for?

Job Hunter: I've done demo projects for a number of local musicians.

Interviewer: How many?

Job Hunter: Half a dozen. I also produced an album of my own material, which is instrumentals and vocals with an acoustic guitar.

What to write down:
- Built multitrack home sound recording and video studio.
- Used it to record demo projects for six local musical groups.
- Also self-produced own album, featuring original compositions on an acoustic guitar.

Finally, let's go on to the interests fact sheet.

Interviewer guideline: Aim for specifics about the interests the job hunter has listed and find out whether he or she has only a passing familiarity with them (in which case, they shouldn't be mentioned) or a genuine passion or involvement.

Time for this exercise:
5 minutes

Interests Questions

- What exactly is your involvement with (the interests listed)?
- How much do you know about it?
- How often do you do it?

• • • •

SAMPLE CONVERSATION

Interviewer: What kind of photography do you like to do?

Job Hunter: Mostly candid shots of interesting people I see on the street. I use black-and-white film, not color.

Interviewer: How long have you been doing it?

Job Hunter: For about ten years. I've taken about a dozen photography workshops.

Interviewer: Do you do your own developing?

Job Hunter: I develop and print my own pictures.

What to write down:
- Take black-and-white candid shots of people.
- Develop and print own pictures.

Time for this exercise: Total time:
10 minutes   50 minutes

Selecting a Format

The next step is to decide what kind of format best suits your purpose. (The interviewer can take a break or think through this next step with you.) There are three basic types:

- Chronological—arranging your work experience beginning with your current or most recent job (or school, if you're a student or recent graduate) and working back from there, ultimately listing your first job last
- Functional—organizing your skills, talents, and work experience by major areas of involvement
- Analytical—presenting your background in terms of skills and accomplishments

Chronological

Most people opt for the chronological format because employers find it easy to read and interpret—job titles, the names of employers, and dates of employment stand out. A chronological format should definitely be your choice if:

- You've worked for employers likely to be known to the people who will be reviewing your resume.
- You're applying for a job in a conservative field such as banking, accounting, or law.

- You've been working in one field throughout your career and plan to look for your next position in the same field.

Sequence Suggestion

If you are currently employed:

- Identification
- Work Experience
- Activities and Professional Affiliations
- Education
- Interests

If you are a student or recent graduate:

- Identification
- Education
- Activities or Work Experience (whichever relates more to the kind of job you're applying for)
- Interests

If you are currently employed but are a part-time student:

- Identification
- Work Experience or Education (whichever relates more to the kind of job you're applying for)
- Activities
- Interests

SAMPLE CHRONOLOGICAL RESUME

Ellen Baxter majored in genetics in college and has been working in laboratories full-time since she graduated in 1983. She'd like to become a laboratory manager at a facility bigger than the one she works in now. Her choice of the chronological resume format emphasizes her experiences as a manager of people, resources, and money.

Ellen Baxter
305 Channing Way
Berkeley, California 94704
(415) 555-0985

WORK EXPERIENCE: <u>Laboratory Manager</u>, Biotech Corporation, 1985–present

— Coordinate purchasing of $100,000 worth of supplies and equipment annually
— Direct the work of ten technicians, who were working on separate but related projects
— Developed new recruiting program that doubled the number of qualified applicants and has resulted in at least two new hires annually

<u>Assistant Laboratory Manager</u>, JDL Laboratories, 1983–85

— Researched new lab equipment totaling $50,000, which was subsequently approved and purchased
— Managed office staff of three; developed new personnel performance evaluation, which was adopted
— Helped plan schedules for research work projects

<u>Laboratory Assistant</u>, Genetics Laboratory, University of California at Berkeley, 1980–83
— Prepared media and solutions, which involved use of pH meter
— Cared for lab animals
— Conducted supply and chemical inventories

EDUCATION: B.A., Genetics, University of California at Berkeley, 1983, cum laude

ACTIVITIES: Genetics Association—1982–present—As coordinator of the speakers' forum for the last two years, researched and contacted prominent scientists within state to participate in ten panel discussions, two of which were covered by local media

INTERESTS: Tennis (captain of women's collegiate team), sailing (teach classes to beginners on weekends), and photography (have won two prizes in amateur competitions)

Functional

If you feel that it's important to emphasize areas of expertise, skills, or knowledge, a functional format is a good choice. Because you've identified the job functions in which you excel, employers can immediately get a handle on whether your experience matches their job requirements. What is less apparent in this format is where you acquired and practiced a particular job skill (the job history section lists only job title, name of employer, and dates of employment). You can elaborate more on what you did where in a cover letter or at a job interview.

A functional format makes sense if:

- Your background is a patchwork of education, work, and volunteer experiences.
- You're hoping to change careers and need to transfer skills learned in one profession to a new one.
- You have little or no job experience but have proven your competence in school, volunteer, home, or internship situations.

Sequence Suggestion

- Identification
- Areas of Expertise, Skills, or Knowledge
- Work Experience
- Education
- Interests

SAMPLE FUNCTIONAL RESUME

Jason Snyder would like to land a position with a public relations firm that specializes in politics or with a lobbying organization. Because he developed the skills he needs to do that kind of work in two different jobs—political fund-raising and on the staff of a university—he felt he could more effectively sell himself as a candidate with a functional resume that emphasized his fund-raising, administrative, and managerial experience.

Jason Snyder

38-49 Crescent Street   Phone: (216) 555-9854
Bay Village, Ohio 44035

SKILLS

Fund-Raising: Helped solicit funds in successful Ohio 1986
gubernatorial campaign
Prepared rationale for financial assistance for health
fairs and conferences
Participated in numerous telethons sponsored by
university alumni department; personally raised
$500,000 in pledges

Administration: Planned various conference dates, locations, facilities;
organized schedule of events
Devised automated office systems, particularly database
mailing systems
Computed budgets for departments with as many as
fifty staff members

Management: Mobilized volunteers and coordinated their work at
conferences
Devised system for collection, organization, and
dissemination of information to student body of
35,000

WORK EXPERIENCE

Office Manager, Ohio Gubernatorial Fund Raising, 1986–88

Director, Student Department of International Affairs, Case Western
Reserve University, 1985

Coordinator, Cuyahoga, Ohio, Health Fair, 1984

EDUCATION

Bachelor of Arts, Speech Communication, Case Western Reserve
University, 1984

Graduated magna cum laude, earned 80 percent of expenses

INTERESTS

Hiking the Appalachian Trail, speaking to grade school students
about electoral politics

Analytical

In an analytical format, you present what you know and what you've done not as job descriptions (the case in chronological resumes) or descriptions of areas of expertise (the case in functional resumes) but as individual skills and achievements. As such, you might want to select the headings "Capabilities" or "Expertise" rather than "Skills," and "Accomplishments" rather than "Achievements." This unconventional type of resume requires a more careful reading by a prospective employer than a chronological or functional resume—your suitability for a position may not be readily apparent from it. Still, it can be the right choice, particularly for:

- People returning to the work force after taking time off for educational, family, personal, or health reasons.
- Military personnel looking for their first civilian job.
- Job hunters who want to shape their experiences to fit a particular kind of position.

Sequence Suggestion

- Identification
- Capabilities, Expertise, or Skills
- Accomplishments or Achievements
- Work History
- Education
- Interests

SAMPLE ANALYTICAL RESUME

Jennifer Langston hoped to get a position in magazine or book publishing after an eight-year editing career in the U.S. Navy. She decided to use the analytical resume format and selected only those skills and capabilities that were related to the job she hoped to get and to list the awards she'd received for top military job performance.

Jennifer Langston
662 S. Emerald Lane
Teaneck, NJ 07666
(201) 555-2903

ACHIEVEMENTS

— Rated top officer in my rank at each command (U.S. Navy)
— Earned seven awards for outstanding performance, including two Navy Commendation Medals for writing and editing publications
— Received personal commendation from one of five top-ranking naval officers for coordinating reports from twenty-one Pentagon staff offices and nine Fleet staffs

CAPABILITIES

— Developed extensive knowledge of writing and editing processes, particularly interpreting technical information and making it understandable to lay audience
— Outlined and wrote speeches for top managers and officers
— Acquired desktop publishing skills to produce professional-quality publications
— Managed staff of fifteen professionals and five office support people

SKILLS

— Solid working knowledge of Pagemaker, Filemaker, and WordPerfect
— Strong proofreading skills
— Electronic database research know-how

WORK EXPERIENCE

— United States Navy, 1980–88
    — Command and Control Center Officer
    — Intelligence Research Analyst
    — Operations Analyst/Briefer

EDUCATION

— Bachelor of Arts, Journalism, Bowling Green State University, 1980

INTERESTS

— Collecting eighteenth- and nineteenth-century toys, going on archaeological digs, singing in choruses

It's Sort and Review Time

If you feel you need a break, take a 5- or 10-minute breather. After snacking on the pizza you ordered earlier, it will be time to organize the notes on your fact sheets.

The interviewer can change hats for this exercise and, with you, select and edit the information that will go on the first draft of your resume. If one of you can type, using a typewriter will speed up the process. Using a computer is even better because you will be able to add and delete information easily. If you have neither, write legibly.

If you've decided on a functional or an analytical format, skip ahead to page 47 for instructions on how to proceed with a functional resume or to page 53 for instructions on producing an analytical resume. Instructions for producing a chronological resume begin on the next page.

Time for this exercise:
30 minutes

Total time:
80 minutes

Going the Chronological Route

For now, put aside the identification fact sheet, which can easily be slotted into any resume design you choose. Let's begin with the work experience fact sheet.

Step One: If you've decided what kind of position you're going to be applying for, put check marks next to the job responsibilities and accomplishments that are strong evidence that you're qualified to do that kind of work. Then decide which jobs you want to provide the most detail about. The ones you choose will probably be those under which you have a lot of check marks. Consider separating the jobs that are directly related to the kind of position you hope to get from other work experiences. The two can be differentiated in your headings—"Retail Experience" and "Other Work Experience," for example.

Step Two: Consolidate your responsibilities and accomplishments at each job into three to five concise statements. Begin each one with an action verb and use past tense (coordinated, not coordinate) for all except your current job (if you still have a particular responsibility, use the present tense). Don't make the verb a noun (negotiation skills instead of negotiate). Don't end the verb with "ing."

Here is a list of synonyms for ten verbs that describe typical job functions. For more help in coming up with descriptive action verbs, consult a thesaurus.

Calculate	**Care for**	**Coordinate**	**Decide**
Analyze	Administer to	Arrange	Determine
Compute	Attend to	Assign	Evaluate
Estimate	Look after	Organize	Judge
Figure	Serve	Regulate	Select
Take account of	Watch over	Systematize	Weigh
Manage	**Market**	**Mediate**	**Route**
Administer	Deal in	Accommodate	Direct
Head	Sell	Bring to terms	Expedite
Lead	Shop	Pacify	Guide
Oversee		Reconcile	Schedule
Supervise		Settle	Track
Train	**Write**		
Coach	Communicate		
Inform	Compile		
Instruct	Compose		
Teach	Draft		
Tutor			

EXAMPLES

What you've written on your work experience fact sheet:

Checked into a dozen news bulletins daily.
Called up sources to verify and add information.
Wrote rough copy for writers and editors to polish.

How to translate it on your resume:

- Researched a dozen news bulletins daily by calling up sources to verify facts and wrote first-draft news stories

What you've written on your work experience fact sheet:	Take phone calls from dissatisfied or confused customers, an average of fifty a day.
	Talk to them without losing my cool.
	Have them talk to my supervisor or write up a report to proper department if I can't help them.
	Have received more than 100 letters thanking me personally for my help last year.

How to translate it on your resume:

- Help an average of fifty customers who call in daily
- Process or refer complex customer complaints through proper channels
- Have received more than 100 thank-you letters from customers citing my helpfulness and courtesy in the last year

Writing Tips

If you're not used to writing on a regular basis, you may find the task of translating the notes from the interview session into the shorthand language of a resume a bit daunting. But don't worry. Think of the process in terms of the several easy-to-follow formulas listed below.

Formula 1

(A) Action verb *plus*
(B) Object or people *plus*
(C) To or for whom; of, on, or from what; by, through, or with what

EXAMPLES

Dispatched---assignments---to security guards

Monitored---market conditions---for Chicago Mer-
cantile Exchange

Cared for---orphaned infant orangutan

Formula 1 is about as simple as you can get. Don't be
afraid to add details if they better explain a job responsibility or accomplishment.

Formula 2

(A) Compound action verbs *plus*
(B) Object quantified and/or described *plus*
(C) To or for whom; of, on, or from what; by, through, or
     with what *plus*
(D) Descriptor

EXAMPLES

Compiled and wrote---three major state and local
news stories---from wire services---for public affairs
program

Drafted---legal memoranda and briefs weekly---for
senior partners---involved in oil and gas matters

Investigated and reported on---potential employ-
ees---for hiring managers---in high-security-clearance
areas

Don't feel confined by these formulas; they're merely
guidelines for getting your words across clearly and simply.

How to Make an Ordinary Job
Sound Important

Most people have held ordinary jobs, that is, jobs in
which the responsibilities don't seem all that important.

But that doesn't mean you can't make what you did—which, if you did a good job, mattered a great deal to your boss and company—*sound* important. It's all in the phrasing. Here are several examples of how it can be done.

EXAMPLES

Laborer, Sonny's Landscaping
— Transported sensitive plants and trees without incurring damage
— Offered tips to customers on how to maintain landscaping
— Scouted location and offered suggestions to customers on placement

Retail clerk, Bloomingdale's
— Rang up between $4,000 and $6,000 in sales transactions daily
— Handled approximately twenty-five customer complaints and returns weekly; usually able to solve without supervisor assistance
— Assisted department managers in buying merchandise and organizing interior displays

Why You Shouldn't Tell White Lies

You may be tempted to inflate your job title, fudge dates of employment, or exaggerate your educational credentials on your resume in order to come across as a more qualified job candidate. It's *not* a good idea.

Altering the truth can get you into trouble. Employers today often take the time to check out information on resumes. If prospective employers discover inconsistencies, they are likely to bump you off the list immediately. The reasoning? If you lie about your credentials, how can you be trusted as an employee? If the discovery is made after you've been hired, you stand to lose your job. In short, the edge you think you may gain isn't worth the risk.

There *are* ways to present yourself as a strong candidate without telling white lies and jeopardizing your credibility, however. Avoid the temptations listed below by following the accompanying suggestions.

- *Stretching dates of employment.* If you want to disguise a period in which you were unemployed—at least until you can explain the situation in person—one solution is to drop the months from employment dates and use just years. If, however, you did not work for one or more years because you took time off for child rearing, health problems, or other personal reasons, you're probably best off explaining the gap in your cover letter.
- *Changing job titles.* The risk of changing your real title to make it more prestigious is that you're likely to be caught. It's one of the few things that personnel departments routinely provide to prospective employers who inquire. You're better off communicating the important role you played by emphasizing the responsibilities you held that went beyond your job description. If you were a legal secretary, for example, mention the number of times you filed papers in court on behalf of your boss rather than saying you were a paralegal.
- *Inventing academic credentials.* It's downright dangerous to claim you attended or graduated from a particular school if you didn't—just as bad is awarding yourself a degree you never earned. If a help-wanted ad or posted job requires a certain educational background, be honest about your credentials and explain in your cover letter why you should nonetheless be considered.
- *Exaggerating your capabilities.* Being self-confident is a plus, but overstating your knowledge or expertise on paper not only may cause embarrassment if you're asked a technical question during the interview but may result in your being written off as a fraud.

- *Taking more credit than is yours.* It's fine to describe your contributions to a successful project, but saying that you initiated, supervised, or were solely responsible for something when that was not really the case is foolish. It's too easy for a prospective employer to discover what your real role was through a conversation with your former boss, colleagues, or people you both know. At the very least, your credibility will suffer; and in the worst-case scenario, you'll be dismissed as a candidate.
- *Claiming free-lance or consultant status.* You should claim such status only if you really were engaged in such efforts; otherwise, you won't have legitimate answers about questions an employer is likely to ask about your "business."

Pulling It Together

If you hope to get your resume on one page (a good idea for most people), you probably won't have space to describe more than five jobs—describing three or four is preferable. That means simply listing or eliminating less important ones. Unless they're related to your job objective, summer, part-time, or preprofessional jobs, or ones that don't require explanation, should be the first to go. You can always create an "Additional Work Experience" category if you feel strongly about mentioning them.

EXAMPLE

Additional Work Experience:	Swimming instructor (summers during college)
	Waitress (part-time during school year)
	French tutor, teacher's aide

A word of advice: As you and the interviewer review the edited information, make sure that it is clear and contains both accomplishments and responsibilities—and as many numbers as make sense!

Step Three: Let's move on to your education fact sheet. Unless you're a student or recent graduate, this information should be a cinch to arrange. The longer you've been out in the work world, the less space should be devoted to this section, which should follow the experience section. If you've been out three or more years, it's necessary to include only the name of your school(s), year of graduation, degree, and academic honors.

Recent graduates and currently enrolled students should follow these general organizational guidelines: Your education section should follow the identification section. After the heading, put the name of the degree or certificate you received followed by your major or program of study, the name of the school and month and year your degree was (or will be) received, and any academic honors. If necessary, briefly describe the program.

EXAMPLES

College graduate:	Bachelor of Science, Biology, Rutgers University, May 1988, cum laude
Professional:	Diploma Program in Personnel Management, New York University, December 1987, a 16-credit advanced professional program
High school graduate:	Graduate, Bay Shore High School, June 1988, GPA 3.45

Subheadings under education might include Honors (or Awards or Recognition), Special Training (or Courses, Concentration, or Programs of Study), Thesis or Research Topic, and Scholarships. If you can get the information across in a few words, that's great.

EXAMPLES

Honors:	Law Review
Concentration:	Financial management of nonprofit organizations
Scholarship:	Four-year full tuition scholarship

If the additional information requires more than a few words to be meaningful, try to be as succinct as possible.

EXAMPLE

What you wrote on your education fact sheet:	Wrote one of ten best senior term papers. Nominated by history professor. Selected by a faculty committee from a field of 20 finalists and over 300 entrants.

How to translate it on your resume:

- Wrote history term paper, which was 1 of 10 (out of 300) selected by faculty as best senior term papers

If you paid for some or all of your education, you can add the following notation:

- Worked part-time and summers to pay for 75 percent of college expenses

Step Four: You're now ready to edit the activities fact sheet. Decide first which heading is most appropriate, given the kind of information you're presenting. Possibilities include:

- Professional Affiliations
- Community or Civic Activities
- Volunteer Work
- Extracurricular Activities

One of the best ways to give a capsule view of your involvement is to list the type of affiliation you have (member, officer, or committee head), the name of the organization, and the date you joined (1985 to present, for example) or, if you are no longer affiliated, the dates of your involvement.

If your contributions or time involvement with a particular organization were significant or relate to the kinds of experience you'll need to get the job you want, describe your accomplishments or the skills you developed. You can use the same writing formulas to describe them as you used to describe your job responsibilities and accomplishments.

EXAMPLES

Extracurricular Activities:
- Built multitrack home sound recording and video studio.
- Recorded demo projects for six local musical groups and self-produced album, featuring original compositions on an acoustic guitar.

Professional Affiliation:
Regional chair, American Psychological Association, 1987–88

Community Activities:
Organizer, 96th Street Block Association Recycling Project, 1987–present
—Presented plan accepted by officers to fund education kits for twenty-five member buildings
—Recruited ten building captains to coordinate recycling efforts
—Reduced trash removal by 15 percent in first year and 25 percent in second

> and generated $1,000
> from recyclable waste,
> which paid for pickup
> costs and a $500 contri-
> bution to the Central
> Park Conservancy

Step Five: Finally, let's work on your interests fact sheet. A simple list, even if it consists of only two items, is fine, but it's important that it be specific. Saying that you like sports, reading, or traveling isn't very telling. If you have space, include a brief description after the interest. You don't need to use action verbs—nouns (coin collecting) are fine; so are gerunds (collecting coins).

EXAMPLES

Karate (have earned a yellow belt)

Playing the piano (have a regular one-night engagement each weekend at a local restaurant)

Black-and-white photography (develop and print own photos)

Or you can incorporate a brief description by using more than one word to describe the interest.

EXAMPLES

Collecting antique Christmas ornaments

Building grandfather clocks

Running 10K races

Refining Your Draft

If you didn't go into enough detail during your interview session, it will be evident as you review your resume. If it's too skimpy, you and your interviewer should conduct another fact-finding interview for any category you believe needs more detail. No matter what your background, there are always plenty of details about the kind of work or schooling you've had that are worth highlighting for prospective employers. Keep talking until you uncover them.

If your resume is likely to run more than a page, consider eliminating the oldest jobs or condensing the descriptions under jobs unrelated to your current ambition. Remember, you can simply list part-time, summer, or less important jobs under the heading "Additional Work Experience" and delete the job descriptions under them.

In either case, tighten up the draft by eliminating unnecessary words and information. If you've used any of the following words and phrases, delete them:

- Responsible for
- Involved in
- Experienced in
- Know how to
- Worked as a (job title)
- Conversant in (or with)

Now you're ready to move on to "Perfecting Your Resume" on page 57.

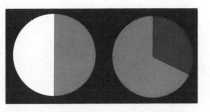

Time for this exercise: Total time:
30 minutes   80 minutes

Choosing a Functional Format

If you decide to go with a functional resume, your biggest decision will be selecting the areas of experience to highlight. If you start by doing Steps Two and Four under the chronological format (pages 35 and 43, respectively), you'll more easily be able to spot similarities among the skills, areas of responsibility, and expertise or knowledge you've acquired in the jobs you've held and the activities you've participated in.

Once you've defined your categories, select the descriptions of responsibilities or accomplishments from each job you've held or activity you've participated in and put each one under the proper category. Feel free both to eliminate job descriptions, accomplishments, or activities that don't relate to the kind of job you hope to land and to insert additional points if you feel they're necessary.

EXAMPLE

Janet Forrester has held administrative and teaching jobs at one college since receiving her master's degree from the institution in 1984. She now wants to look for a job in event coordination, possibly with a corporation or meeting planning organization. She developed this profile by following Steps Two and Four from the chronological resume instructions:

Indiana University, Bloomington, Indiana, 1984–present

College Adviser, 1986–present

— Help 150 freshmen plan their curricula
— Initiate tutoring program for students on academic probation
— Coordinate ten major freshman events, including Freshman Family Day, Opening Day Activities, and Freshman Orientation

Program Assistant, Arts and Sciences Division, 1985–86

— Organized faculty committee to review goals and objectives of core curriculum
— Conducted curriculum update workshops for faculty advisers
— Wrote new course catalog for students studying abroad

Instructor, English Department, 1984–85

— Developed and taught remedial writing course, which received faculty recognition at an honors banquet
— Supervised three teaching assistants who graded freshman compositions

Faculty Adviser, Student Activities Office, 1984–85

— Reviewed decisions of elected student officers on bookings of entertainment and cultural events for campus
— Monitored expenditures of $500,000 of student activity fee money

Janet realized that she had experience in four skill areas that related to her next career goal—communications, event coordination, management, and planning. She rearranged the descriptions under her jobs to fit the appropriate categories. (Note: For consistency, it's best to use the past tense of all action verbs, even for current job responsibilities, in the functional format.)

Communications

— Wrote new course catalog for students studying abroad
— Developed and taught remedial writing course, which received faculty recognition at an honors banquet
— Conducted curriculum update workshops for faculty advisers

Event Coordination

— Coordinated ten major freshman events, including Freshman Family Day, Opening Day Activities, and Freshman Orientation
— Organized faculty committee to review goals and objectives of core curriculum

Management

— Supervised three teaching assistants who graded freshman compositions
— Reviewed decisions of elected student officers on bookings of entertainment and cultural events for campus
— Monitored expenditures of $500,000 of student activity fee money

Planning

— Helped 150 freshmen plan their curricula
— Initiated tutoring program for students on academic probation

If you want to include skills or experience you've gained outside of the jobs you've held, consult your education and activities fact sheets. You might need to add *who, what, when,* and *where* to explain the context in which you performed a particular function.

EXAMPLE

Fund-raising:

— *As a committee head of local chapter of Amnesty International,* coordinated activities of five people who produced benefit chamber music concert—raised $10,000

— *As vice president of alumni association,* built alumni database and outreach program that resulted in 100 percent increase in annual contributions

Three categories, each containing three to five points, work well on a functional resume, although four or five categories are acceptable.

Next, transfer the bare-boned details of your work history from your work experience fact sheet into a section you might call "Employment" or "Work History." Most prospective employers want to know dates, so it's best to include them along with the name of the employer. If you want to deemphasize the fact that you changed jobs frequently or if there are gaps in your work experience, use years of employment rather than months and years, as noted earlier. Or you can group employers and years of employment in a more general way.

EXAMPLE

1975–88   — Worked as a secretary for small and medium-sized law firms, including Alexander & Ward, Jacobson and Levy, and Millar, Gordon & Beckett.

While you don't have to include a job title, it does give the reader some sense of your job level, at least on your last job. But be sure to include titles if they are in some way prestigious or show you were promoted.

If you changed jobs frequently or have gaps in your work history, be prepared to answer a prospective employer's likely question: "Why?"

Follow Step Three from the chronological format to develop your education section and Step Five to conclude with your interests section (pages 42 and 45, respectively). If you have information from your activities fact sheet that you weren't able to incorporate under your major skill category headings, you may want to create one more section to list them. Again, choose a heading that best fits, for example, "Professional Affiliations." This section can follow your work experience or education section—wherever you and your interviewer think it fits best.

Once you've organized your information, you and your interviewer should review it to make sure that each category makes sense and presents a clear picture of your knowledge and expertise within each functional area. Refer back to the "Refining Your Draft" section on page 45 before you move on to "Perfecting Your Resume" on page 57.

Time for this exercise: Total time:
30 minutes   80 minutes

Producing the Analytical Resume

Putting together an analytical resume is a bit more challenging than the more conventional chronological and functional resumes. Why? Because you selectively include information from your fact sheets that fits the categories of the analytical format: "Abilities," "Capabilities," or "Expertise," and "Accomplishments" or "Achievements."

The best way to start is to put your work experience, education, and activities fact sheets side by side. Go over each and put a check mark next to any note that could be called a result or an accomplishment. Entries that include numbers are prime candidates for consideration, and you are likely to find good material in your responses to the questions:

- Did any of your accomplishments ever result in a promotion, raise, or other type of recognition?
- How were you selected for the honor you've listed under education?
- Were you involved in any special activities, committees, or fund-raising as a member?

All the points you've checked are potential items to include under the "Accomplishments" or "Achievements" section.

Next, mark with plus signs those points on each of the three fact sheets that could best be called abilities. Keep in mind that an ability is something that you do well even though you may not have had specific experience using it in a paying job. It may be your ability to manage income and expenses for rental properties you or your family owns, repair foreign car engines, or use computer databases to do research. These could work well under the section you've labeled "Abilities," "Capabilities," or "Expertise."

You should come up with a minimum of five accomplishments and five abilities. If you're applying for a particular kind of job, be sure the ones you select provide evidence of your credentials to handle it.

Finally, you may want to create a "Skills" section to provide information that wasn't appropriate to include under the other two categories. The difference between a skill and an ability is that a skill is good working knowledge of a specific task, tool, or system, while an ability is experience in a particular functional area. For example, a paralegal may know how to do legal research (an ability) and may also know how to use the computerized legal database LEXIS (a skill). Check your work experience, activities, and education fact sheets for skills you may have developed through your work in organizations or courses of study.

EXAMPLE

Ted Clarkins is a skiing enthusiast who, since graduating from college, worked for ten years as a waiter and bartender at ski resorts. He has decided to get serious and begin a career with a major hotel or restaurant chain. He chose the analytical resume format as the best way to sell himself. Here's a polished version of information from his fact sheets:

Work Experience Fact Sheet

- Developed extensive knowledge of food and beverage operations at a variety of restaurants, ranging from fast-food to three-star establishments

- Understand how to balance service, production, and style
- Cited consistently by supervisors as "one of the hardest-working servers or bartenders" they've ever had
- Trained at least fifty bartenders-in-training and twenty-five servers to perform their job tasks
- Acted as beverage purchasing agent and learned pricing and inventory control
- Won recognition as "Employee of the Month" from five different restaurants
- Gained experience in crisis management while filling in for managers on several dozen occasions

Activities Fact Sheet

- Appointed head of a twenty-five-member ski patrol on the basis of management and interpersonal skills
- Taught more than fifty skiers patrol, rescue, and emergency first-aid techniques
- Saved the lives of three skiers trapped in an avalanche
- Managed the scheduling of three shifts of twenty-five-member ski patrol

Here's how Ted organized the information into an analytical resume.

Capabilities

- Developed extensive knowledge of food and beverage operations at a variety of restaurants, ranging from fast-food to three-star establishments
- Understand how to balance service, production, and style
- Developed effective training techniques—trained at least fifty bartenders-in-training and twenty-five servers to perform job tasks and taught more than fifty skiers patrol, rescue, and emergency first-aid techniques

- Acted as beverage purchasing agent and learned pricing and inventory control
- Gained experience in crisis management while filling in for managers on several dozen occasions
- Managed the scheduling of three shifts of twenty-five-member ski patrol

Accomplishments

- Cited consistently by supervisors as "one of the hardest-working servers or bartenders" they've ever had
- Won recognition as "Employee of the Month" from five different restaurants
- Appointed head of a twenty-five-member ski patrol on the basis of management and interpersonal skills
- Saved the lives of three skiers trapped in an avalanche

It's advisable to include a summary of your work history and education—employers usually want to know how many jobs you've held as well as when and where you worked in them. Read over the suggestions on page 47 under "Choosing a Functional Format" to develop these sections.

Once you've added these last two sections, follow the final directions in "Refining Your Draft" on page 45.

Time for this exercise:
5 minutes

Total time:
85 minutes

Perfecting Your Resume

The final step before choosing a layout is to edit your draft to make sure that you haven't forgotten any critical piece of information, however small, and to make sure that it reads clearly and logically. The following checklist can help you do that:

1. Are all the elements of the identification correct and complete?

2. Do you want to add a job objective? (Since job objective statements must be specific to be effective, they're worth including only if you intend to apply for a particular kind of position. Job objectives are more often found on functional and analytical resumes. Remember, a job objective can just as easily be mentioned in a cover letter.)

EXAMPLE

Job Objective: A position as manager of the word processing staff of a major law firm

3. Are your headings clear and in the proper order? (If you're unsure, check the Sequence Suggestions on pages 26, 28, and 30, respectively, for the chronological, functional, and analytical resume formats.)

4. Do the points under each section start off with an action verb if possible? Are they clear, concise, and in the appropriate section?

5. Are all major relevant points from your fact sheets covered in some way? (If you want to include a point that doesn't seem to fit under any section, you might want to include it in a cover letter or put it under a section called "Additional Information," which would precede the "Interests" section.)

A Note on References

It's not necessary to include the names, addresses, and phone numbers of past employers or others who are willing to put in a good word for you, nor do you need to state "References available on request." What you may want to do, however, is to prepare such a list on a separate sheet so that you can give it to prospective employers once they indicate you're in the running for the job. (That could be as early as the end of a first interview, which is a good reason to take a reference sheet with you.) A reference sheet should contain the following information for each reference you list: the name of your immediate supervisor, his or her title, phone number, and the name and address of the company.

EXAMPLE

Andrew Amore

List of References
Robert Johnson, Vice President, Taxes
Sara Lee Corporation
Three First National Plaza
Chicago, Illinois 60604
312-555-2600

Lynn Adams, Vice President, Finance
Sara Lee Corporation
Three First National Plaza
Chicago, Illinois 60604
312-555-2600

Hope Dunfrey, Tax Manager
PepsiCo, Inc.
700 Anderson Hill Road
Purchase, New York 10577
914-555-2000

Max Sherman, Partner
Arthur Andersen & Co.
301 East 9th Street
Cleveland, Ohio 43205
216-555-9070

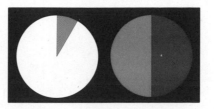

Selecting the Right Design

What your resume says is important, but unless it looks inviting, it may not get more than a glance from a potential employer. You don't have to have design experience to make your resume pleasing to the eye, but be aware that it should contain the following elements:

- *White space.* Margins left and right as well as top and bottom and space in between sections should be included.
- *Placement of headings.* Arrange headings so they can easily be identified.
- *Consistent typefaces.* Individual elements such as headings, job titles, or employers should be treated in the same way.
- *Proper indentations.* Headings, points, and sub-points should line up.
- *Graphic elements.* Bullets, dashes, and rules should be used for ease of reading.

You may choose to select one of the following designs for your resume or to modify one to meet your specific needs. The only way you'll know for sure whether or not your information fits a particular design is to type up one or more versions using different margins and spacing. (If you're using a computer, you may want to experiment with different typefaces.) The time required to type your resume is not included in the suggested 5 minutes, since typing skills vary widely. If you don't have access to a typewriter, print a version that's legible, and clearly mark for the typist what you'd like boldfaced, italicized, capitalized, indented, or underlined. Keep in mind that you can emphasize sections of your resume by using the design elements described earlier.

Here are nine resume designs—five for the chronological format, two for the functional format, and two for the analytical format. You can borrow section elements from any of the samples to put together your own unique look.

Chronological Format Design

EXAMPLE ONE

YOUR NAME   Street address, city, state, zip code, phone number

EXPERIENCE: *Job title,* place of employment, dates of employment

— Job responsibility or accomplishment
— Job responsibility or accomplishment
— Job responsibility or accomplishment

Job title, place of employment, dates of employment

— Job responsibility or accomplishment
— Job responsibility or accomplishment
— Job responsibility or accomplishment

Job title, place of employment, dates of employment

— Job responsibility or accomplishment
— Job responsibility or accomplishment

EDUCATION: *Name of degree,* name of school, date of graduation

ACTIVITIES: *Member or officer,* name of organization, dates of involvement

— Description of activity, role, accomplishment

INTERESTS: Activity and brief description, activity and brief description

Chronological Format Design

EXAMPLE TWO

YOUR NAME

Temporary street address   Permanent street address
City, state, zip code   City, state, zip code
Phone number   Phone number

EDUCATION

Name of degree, name of school, date of graduation
Name of degree, name of school, date of graduation

PROFESSIONAL EXPERIENCE

Place of employment, dates of employment

  Job Title:

                Job responsibility or accomplishment
                Job responsibility or accomplishment
                Job responsibility or accomplishment

Place of employment, dates of employment

  Job Title:

                Job responsibility or accomplishment
                Job responsibility or accomplishment
                Job responsibility or accomplishment

OTHER WORK EXPERIENCE

Worked as a job title, job title, job title for various employers on a
part-time basis during the school year

EXTRACURRICULAR ACTIVITIES

Name of club, type of involvement, dates of involvement
Name of club, type of involvement, dates of involvement

Chronological Format Design

EXAMPLE THREE

YOUR NAME
Street address
City, state, zip code
Office phone number
Answering machine number

WORK EXPERIENCE

Month/year to   **Job title.** Name of employer. Location.
month/year   Description of job responsibility or accomplishment
Description of job responsibility or accomplishment
Description of job responsibility or accomplishment
Description of job responsibility or accomplishment

Month/year to   **Job title.** Name of employer. Location.
month/year   Description of job responsibility or accomplishment
Description of job responsibility or accomplishment
Description of job responsibility or accomplishment
Description of job responsibility or accomplishment

Month/year to   **Job title.** Name of employer. Location.
month/year   Description of job responsibility or accomplishment
Description of job responsibility or accomplishment
Description of job responsibility or accomplishment
Description of job responsibility or accomplishment

EDUCATION   Date degree received. Name of degree. Major. Name
of college. Honors.

ACTIVITIES   Description of activity or accomplishment
Description of activity or accomplishment

INTERESTS   Name of activity, name of activity, name of activity

Chronological Format Design

EXAMPLE FOUR

YOUR NAME

Temporary street address   Permanent street address
City, state, zip code   City, state, zip code
Phone number   Phone number
(Until month/year)

OBJECTIVE: Short description

EDUCATION: Name of school, name of degree, major, minor, date
                 received
                 Scholarship, brief description

INTERNSHIPS: Name of employer, brief description of company
                     Dates of employment

                     Job responsibility or accomplishment
                     Job responsibility or accomplishment
                     Job responsibility or accomplishment

                 Name of employer, brief description of company
                     Dates of employment

                     Job responsibility or accomplishment
                     Job responsibility or accomplishment

SUMMER JOBS: Name of employer, job title, dates of employment
                 Name of employer, job title, dates of employment
                 Name of employer, job title, dates of employment

VOLUNTEER   Name of organization, your role or responsibility
WORK: Name of organization, your role or responsibility

PERSONAL   Brief description, brief description, brief description
INTERESTS:

Chronological Format Design

EXAMPLE FIVE

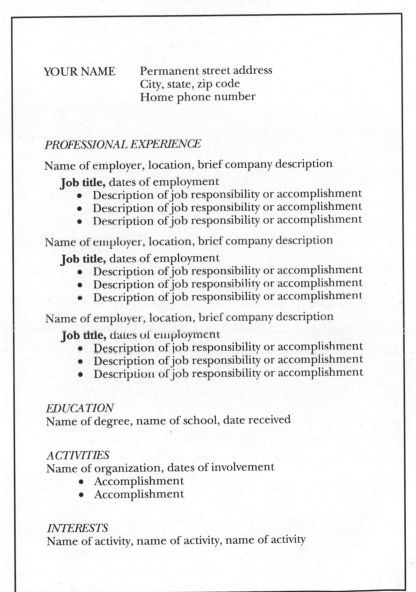

YOUR NAME   Permanent street address
City, state, zip code
Home phone number

PROFESSIONAL EXPERIENCE

Name of employer, location, brief company description

Job title, dates of employment
- Description of job responsibility or accomplishment
- Description of job responsibility or accomplishment
- Description of job responsibility or accomplishment

Name of employer, location, brief company description

Job title, dates of employment
- Description of job responsibility or accomplishment
- Description of job responsibility or accomplishment
- Description of job responsibility or accomplishment

Name of employer, location, brief company description

Job title, dates of employment
- Description of job responsibility or accomplishment
- Description of job responsibility or accomplishment
- Description of job responsibility or accomplishment

EDUCATION
Name of degree, name of school, date received

ACTIVITIES
Name of organization, dates of involvement
- Accomplishment
- Accomplishment

INTERESTS
Name of activity, name of activity, name of activity

Functional Format Design

EXAMPLE ONE

Your Name
Street address
City, state, zip code
Phone number

CATEGORY OF EXPERIENCE

— Description of skill, responsibility, or accomplishment
— Description of skill, responsibility, or accomplishment
— Description of skill, responsibility, or accomplishment

CATEGORY OF EXPERIENCE

— Description of skill, responsibility, or accomplishment
— Description of skill, responsibility, or accomplishment
— Description of skill, responsibility, or accomplishment

CATEGORY OF EXPERIENCE

— Description of skill, responsibility, or accomplishment
— Description of skill, responsibility, or accomplishment
— Description of skill, responsibility, or accomplishment

SKILLS

— Brief description
— Brief description
— Brief description

WORK HISTORY

— Name of employer, job title, dates of employment
— Name of employer, job title, dates of employment
— Name of employer, job title, dates of employment

INTERESTS

— Name of activity, name of activity, name of activity

Functional Format Design

EXAMPLE TWO

YOUR NAME

Temporary street address   Permanent street address
City, state, zip code   City, state, zip code
Phone number   Phone number

EXPERIENCE

CATEGORY OF EXPERIENCE
- Description of skill, responsibility, or accomplishment
- Description of skill, responsibility, or accomplishment
- Description of skill, responsibility, or accomplishment

CATEGORY OF EXPERIENCE
- Description of skill, responsibility, or accomplishment
- Description of skill, responsibility, or accomplishment
- Description of skill, responsibility, or accomplishment

CATEGORY OF EXPERIENCE
- Description of skill, responsibility, or accomplishment
- Description of skill, responsibility, or accomplishment
- Description of skill, responsibility, or accomplishment

WORK HISTORY

- Job title, name of employer, dates of employment
- Job title, name of employer, dates of employment
- Job title, name of employer, dates of employment
- Job title, name of employer, dates of employment

EDUCATION

- Name of program, name of school, dates attended

INTERESTS

Name of activity and/or brief description
Name of activity and/or brief description

Analytical Format Design

EXAMPLE ONE

Your Name
Street address
City, state, zip code
Phone number

*Abilities*_____

    Description of ability
    Description of ability
    Description of ability
    Description of ability

*Accomplishments*_____

    Description of accomplishment
    Description of accomplishment
    Description of accomplishment

*Employment History*_____

    Job title, name of employer, dates of employment
    Job title, name of employer, dates of employment
    Job title, name of employer, dates of employment

*Education*_____

    Name of degree, name of school, date of graduation
        —Special course work

*Interests*_____

    Name of activity, name of activity, name of activity

Analytical Format Design

EXAMPLE TWO

Your Name	Street address, city, state, zip code Phone number
Job Objective	Brief description
Education	Name of college, degree received, date of degree
Achievements	Description of achievement Description of achievement Description of achievement Description of achievement
Capabilities	Description of capability Description of capability Description of capability Description of capability Description of capability Description of capability
Special Skills	Name of skill, name of skill, name of skill
Work Experience	Name of employer, job title, dates of employment Name of employer, job title, dates of employment Name of employer, job title, dates of employment
Interests	Brief description, brief description

The Final Version

Now that you have completed the last session of the 90-minute program, you're ready to produce the final version of your resume. If you don't have a typewriter that can generate a clean copy, it's worthwhile to find one that does, even if it requires hiring a professional typist. The more sophisticated the typewriter, the more options you'll have with type styles. If you have access to a computer or take your resume to a photocopy/print shop, you'll have even more choices. Before your resume is reproduced, you and at least one other person should give it a final proofreading so that no spelling errors or typos sneak through. If you're using a computer, run a spelling check.

It's fine to reproduce your resume on white paper, but avoid cheap-looking copier paper or erasable paper, which can smudge. If you want your resume to withstand heavy handling, get a bond paper with cotton fiber—25 percent or even 50 percent. You can add "weight" to your resume by selecting a 20- or 24-pound paper. And you can add class with a woven rather than smooth finish. For color, stick to tones of white, beige, or gray. A pastel may distinguish your resume from others, but not in the right way.

Revising Your Resume

If you already have a resume—even if it is a few years old—you might want to start with a revision of that version rather than start from scratch, unless you're considering switching formats (see the section "Selecting a Format," on page 25). If you decide to change formats, you may want to follow all the steps recommended for the "from scratch" resume and use information from your current resume to give you a head start with your fact sheets. In either case, however, start with this checklist:

— Delete "Resume" or "Resume of" heading
— Eliminate any personal information other than name, address, and phone number
— Decide whether a job objective is really necessary (see point 2 under "Perfecting Your Resume" on page 57)
— Evaluate the order of your headings (see the sequences suggested under the "Selecting a Format" section beginning on page 26)
— Substitute "responsible for"s with action verbs

Next, critique your content. The biggest weakness of most chronological resumes is lackluster and/or unclear job descriptions. If that's what you've found, you probably never focused on what you did in those positions that was special. Go back to the "Ready, Set, Start the Interview" section on page 15.

> *Interviewer guideline:* Ask the questions that appear under the work experience fact sheet section. Keep in mind that the job hunter's current resume may reflect answers only to the first question rather than to subsequent ones. Your job is to get the job hunter to focus on his or her accomplishments and skills.

Now, jump ahead to the "Going the Chronological Route" section on page 35 and follow Steps One and Two. When you complete them, your work experience section should be considerably stronger. If the descriptions under each job are too long, consider which responsibilities—or jobs—are worth deleting or abbreviating.

If you want to strengthen other sections of your resume, have your interviewer ask you the questions for those sections to generate new or better information. Follow the editing suggestions under "Refining Your Draft" on page 45.

Consider taking your resume revision one step further by evaluating its design. Read "Selecting the Right Design" on page 61 for tips on how to improve it, then follow the instructions in "The Final Version" on page 73.

EXAMPLE

Jacqueline Lionel has been working in advertising and marketing for ten years but hadn't updated her resume in three. Deciding to do something about that, she had a friend play the role of interviewer to help her strengthen her work experience section; she had always saved describing her accomplishments until she went on an interview. Here is what her resume looked like before the revision:

Resume of

Jacqueline Lionel
16 Kennedy Way
Cambridge, Massachusetts 02142
(617) 555-2389 (home)

Job History

LLK&D Advertising, Boston, Massachusetts
Assistant Media Planner, 1/83–5/86
   Responsible for preparing rough drafts of client presentations, suggesting ideas for media placement, tracking placement of client advertisements, doing basic financial analyses of client campaigns.

Salesnet, a division of Dun & Bradstreet, Norwalk, Connecticut
Telemarketing Supervisor, 12/81–12/83
   Responsible for training, supervising, and scripting of client calls.
Telemarketing Communicator, 10/80–12/81
   Sold telephone services, equity access accounts, encyclopedias, and children's books; demonstrated telemarketing for major clients; developed scripting of calls.

Education
B.A., Marketing, University of Massachusetts at Amherst, June 1980

Interests
Hang gliding, listening to classical music

Jacqueline incorporated a number of professional achievements that surfaced during the interview with her friend. Because she added her most recent position and expanded the information under her most recent jobs, she abbreviated her position as a telemarketer.

Jacqueline Lionel
16 Kennedy Way
Cambridge, Massachusetts 02142
(617) 555-8770 (office)

Work Experience

LLK&D Advertising, *__Media Planner__*, May 1986 to present
- Plan and implement media activity for five national advertisers, including Coca-Cola, Levi Strauss, and Pillsbury
- Manage annual media budgets of over $75-million
- Devised client presentations that succeeded in attracting three major new advertisers
- Supervise a department of five professionals and two staff members

__Assistant Media Planner__, January 1983 to May 1986
- Started as secretary, but selected for company training program within three months
- Prepared first copy for client presentations
- Researched media placement options, and after one year was allowed to make presentations directly to clients
- Analyzed efficiency of client campaigns using Lotus 1-2-3

Salesnet, a division of Dun & Bradstreet, *__Telemarketing Supervisor__*, December 1981 to December 1983
- Promoted to this position after one year of working as a telemarketing communicator (10/80–12/81)
- Supervised a staff of ten
- Recruited five new hires and trained them in telemarketing
- Developed new scripts which resulted in a 20 percent increase in sale of telephone services

Education

B.A., Marketing, University of Massachusetts at Amherst, June 1980

Interests

Hang gliding, listening to classical music

Revising your resume isn't unlike making improvements in your home—the big ones can change the way you (or your space) will be perceived; the small ones bring your resume (or home) closer to perfection. Most important, you feel more confident because you've made an effort to do the best job possible.

Putting Your Resume to Work for You

By the time you read this section, you should feel a sense of accomplishment. An hour and a half of concentrated effort is hard work, so be sure to reward yourself.

Once the final version is reproduced, you'll be armed with your most important job hunting tool: you. But even the best of resumes won't get you interviews unless you shop it around. Now is the time to start getting your resume out to the employers who advertise in the help-wanted section of your newspaper or to those you choose to contact directly. Don't neglect to send out copies to the people listed below. Why cover such a wide circle? Because you never know who may be the source of the lead that could become your new job.

- *Friends, friends of your parents, neighbors, and relatives.* Sure they know you, but chances are they aren't familiar enough with your work experience to speak knowledgeably about your skills and accomplishments.
- *Ex-colleagues.* Track them down if they've changed employers—they can be one of your biggest sources of job leads.
- *People you know through social, school, athletic, or community organizations.* If they aren't in a position to put you in touch with a job contact, they may know someone who can.

- *Colleagues in professional organizations.* It pays to be discreet if you're job hunting, so you should pass your resume on only to those you can trust to keep it quiet.
- *Alumni resume databanks.* At many colleges and universities, the placement or alumni office tries to link up job hunting alumni with employers.

I'm honored that you took my resume-writing advice to heart, and I promise you this: If you put the same level of concentrated energy into conducting your job search, you'll find a better, perhaps even spectacular, new position.

MORE OUTSTANDING TITLES FROM PETERSON'S

TOP PROFESSIONS
The 100 Most Popular, Dynamic, and Profitable Careers in America Today

Nicholas Basta

Career-minded students and professionals are anxious to know what the job market will hold in the final decade of the twentieth century.

Top Professions provides for those people fresh, realistic guidance on the job market of the 1990s. It not only uncovers promising options but also helps readers capitalize on current business and economic trends in career decision making.

Describing the top careers—from arts and media to engineering sciences—each entry includes:

- Average starting salary range
- Forecast of demand for professionals in the field
- Highlights of entry-level positions
- Contact numbers at professional associations

"At last, a career book that doesn't hash over the stale government advice provided by the Occupational Outlook Handbook! Basta's book covers—with wit and wisdom—the careers that will engage 99% of all new college grads."
—Steven S. Ross
Columbia University

$10.95 paperback

PETERSON'S JOB OPPORTUNITIES 1991

The newest edition of these classic career guides provides crucial information for job seekers in 1991.

Individual employer profiles list the occupational areas available in each discipline, as well as key facts about:

- Majors sought
- Doctoral-level opportunities
- Opportunities for experienced personnel
- Starting locations by city *and* state

Extensive directories make other important information easy to find, including:

- Industry classifications
- Training programs
- International assignments

PETERSON'S JOB OPPORTUNITIES FOR BUSINESS AND LIBERAL ARTS GRADUATES 1991

Details hundreds of organizations that are recruiting employees in the areas of business and management.

Coming in August 1990
$19.95 paperback
$35.95 hardcover

PETERSON'S JOB OPPORTUNITIES FOR ENGINEERING, SCIENCE, AND COMPUTER GRADUATES 1991

Describes about 1,000 manufacturing, research, consulting, and government organizations hiring technical graduates.

Coming in August 1990

$19.95 paperback
$35.95 hardcover

"For those researching employment opportunities in the fields listed . . . these guides are perfect. Recommended for all libraries."
—Reference Book Review

Look for these and other Peterson's titles in your local bookstore